THE LAKERS: Volume I

By Eric Hirsimaki

Mileposts Publishing Company
3963 Dryden Drive
N. Olmsted, Ohio 44070

© 1987 by Eric Hirsimaki. All rights reserved. This book may not be reproduced in whole or in part without permission in writing from the publisher, except in the case of brief quotations used in reviews.

Library of Congress number   87-091264

First Edition

October 1987

Typesetting by Mag-Tape Composition, Inc.
Cleveland, Ohio

Printed by Gray Graphics
Willoughby, Ohio

Color Separations by Action Nicholson Color
Brookpark, Ohio

For my father,

ELI   N.   HIRSIMAKI

INTRODUCTION

This book isn't intended to be the complete history of lake shipping, but rather a means of showing the reader the many boats and fleets that have been active on the lakes in recent years. Much has changed or vanished during the past decade, so perhaps this volume will provide the reader with some historical perspective.

The purpose of this series of books is to provide a pictorial representation of a unique maritime specimen: the Great Lakes *boat*. Note the use of the term *boat* rather than *ship*. The latter is more familiar to the average reader but is a saltwater term that has no application on the great inland sea. Like any region that has developed its own traditions, lakes men call even a new 1,000 footer a *boat*.

This volume is intended to be the first of a series of books which will try to depict as many boats and fleets as possible. However, since we are concentrating on color photography the available subject matter will necessarily be limited to the post-1945 era. These color photographs will allow us to recreate, albeit briefly, an era that has passed. After all, Shenango's green hull, Republic's orange stack and Inland's classy paint scheme deserve proper recognition.

Special thanks have to be given to the many people who were kind enough to share their material with us:

James Bartke	Paul A. Hilston
William D. Carle III.	Christine Rohn Hilston
G. W. Deucher	Mel Schurdell
Bruce Dicken	Jim Semon
Dave Lawler	Tim Slattery
Lloyd D. Lewis	Bob Todten

Lastly, I'd like to note that much of the caption material wasn't the result of my efforts, but rather the Institute for Great Lakes Research at Bowling Green State University. The late Dr. Richard Wright compiled much of the data and the Institute's staff was kind enough to allow me to use it. Thanks must also go to Joan Sweda who fielded my calls for help. I've attempted to update some listings so if there are any errors they are my responsibility.

I hope you enjoy this book, it was a joy to compile.

Eric Hirsimaki
N. Olmsted, Ohio
September 1987

Table of Contents

Page	Subject	Fleet
1	Title Page	
3	Dedication	
4	Introduction	
5-6	Table of Contents	
7-8	The Great Lakes Bulk Freighter	
9	SILVER ISLE	Pioneer Shipping
10	B. F. JONES	Wilson Marine Transit
11	THE WINTER RUN	
12	SEAWAY QUEEN	Upper Lakes Shipping
13	CHARLES E. WILSON	American Steamship
14	RHODE ISLAND	Great Lakes Towing
15	CHARLES M. SCHWAB	Interlake
16	THE CLEVELANDER	City of Cleveland, Ohio
17	COLLISION BEND	
18	UNGAVA TRANSPORT	Halco
19	NORISLE	Owen Sound Transportation
20	WILLIAM A. WHITNEY	Gaelic Towing
21	LAKEWOOD	Erie Sand
22	ALBERT E. HEEKIN	Hanna
23	MERCURY	Cleveland Tankers
24	HENRY LaLIBERTE	Buckeye Steamship
25	SUNRISE IN DULUTH	
26	L. E. BLOCK	Inland Steel
27	WILLIAM J. DeLANCEY	Interlake
28	JOAN M. McCULLOUGH	Soo River
29	ERIE QUEEN	Wasac Waterways
30	WILLIS B. BOYER	Republic Steel
31	LEHIGH	Bethlehem Steel
32	FRONTENAC	Canada Steamship Lines
33	E. M. FORD	Huron Cement
34	BROOKDALE	Westdale
35	CHIEF WAWATAM	Straits Carferry
36	DULUTH HARBOR	
37	HELEN EVANS	Hindman
38	SENATOR OF CANADA	Paterson
39	WILLIAM R. ROESCH	Kinsman
40	ALPENA	Erie Sand
41	ASHLAND	Columbia
42	FORT YORK	Canada Steamship Lines
43	MATTHEW ANDREWS	Hanna
44	EDWARD L. RYERSON	Inland Steel
45	ELMDALE	Redwood Enterprises
46-47	ALGOWEST	Algoma Central Rwy
48	ELTON HOYT 2nd	Interlake
49	GEORGE STEPHENSON	Buckeye
50	EDWARD B. GREENE	Cleveland-Cliffs
51	SHARON	American Steamship
52	WOLVERINE	Columbia
53	GEORGE HINDMAN	Hindman
54	L'ORME #1	Branch Lines
55	RALPH H. WATSON	U. S. Steel
56	G. A. TOMLINSON	Columbia
57	BAYTON	Misener Steamships
58	DES GROSSILIERS	Canadian Coast Guard
59	WILTRANCO I	Escanaba Towing
60-61	JOSEPH H. THOMPSON	Hanna
62	ANCHORED FOR FOG	
63	CANADIAN PROSPECTOR	Upper Lakes Shipping
64	UHLMAN BROTHERS	Kinsman
65	FOLLOW THE LEADER	
66	SOUTH AMERICAN	Duluth, Chicago & G. Bay
67	COURTNEY BURTON	Columbia
68	CHICAGO TRIBUNE	Q&O Transportation
69	LAWRENCECLIFFE HALL	Halco
70	CHI-CHEEMAUN	Ontario Northland
71	JAMES LAUGHLIN	Wilson Marine Transit

Page	Subject	Fleet	Page	Subject	Fleet
72	SPRING FIT-OUT		94	MEDUSA CHALLENGER	Medusa Cement
73	EDNA G	DM&IR Railway	95	GEORGE M. STEINBRENNER	Kinsman
74	WILLIAM G. MATHER	Cleveland Cliffs	96	STUART J. CORT	Bethlehem Steel
75	JEAN PARISIEN	Canada Steamship Lines	97	VIKING	Chessie System RR
76	DIAMOND ALKYLAI	American Steamship	98	WILFRED SYKES	Inland Steel
77	J. N. McWATTERS	Misener Transportation	99	MIDNIGHT PASSAGE	
78	TOM M. GIRDLER	Republic Steel	100	THE INTERNATIONAL	International Harvester
79	DAVID P. THOMPSON	Pioneer Steamship	101	HERBERT C. JACKSON	Interlake
80	ARTHUR B. HOMER	Bethlehem Steel	102	SOODOC	Paterson
81	LAKE NIPIGON	Nipigon Transport	103	CASON J. CALLAWAY	U. S. Steel
82	MANITOULIN	Canada Steamship Lines	104	ROBERT C. NORTON	Columbia
83	McKEE SONS	American Steamship	105	WALTER A. STERLING	Cleveland Cliffs
84	RALPH MISENER	Misener Transportation	106	DAWN OF A NEW DAY	
85	EUGENE M. PARGNY	U. S. Steel	107	TROISDOC	Paterson
86	BENSON FORD	Rouge Steel	108	MARKHAM	Army Corps of Engineers
87	J. A. W. IGLEHART	Huron Cement	109	IRVING S. OLDS	U. S. Steel
88	GEORGE D. GOBLE	Kinsman	110	CITY OF MIDLAND 41	Ann Arbor RR
89	NORTHERN VENTURE	Upper Lakes	111	JOHN P. REISS	Reiss Steamship
90	COL. JAMES M. SCHOONMAKER	Shenango	112	MEETING ABOVE THE SOO	
			113	Map of the Great Lakes	
91	JOHN G. MUNSON	U. S. Steel	114	Key for Captions	
92	BUCKTHORN	U. S. Coast Guard	115-126	Captions	
93	E. J. NEWBERRY		127	Index of Boats	

THE GREAT LAKES BULK FREIGHTER

The majority of the photographs in this book are of a unique type of boat: the Great Lakes straight-deck bulk freighter. Developed during the latter part of the Nineteenth Century, the design has become a trademark of the lakes all over the world. These lake boats, or lakers, are thus as much a part of the heritage of the Great Lakes as LaSalle's *Griffin* or the iron ore they've carried.

The discovery of iron ore in the Lake Superior region and the subsequent development of the mines there after 1850 created a need for boats to haul the ore to the lower lakes where the steel industry was concentrated. Unfortunately, contemporary lake boats were ill-suited for the iron ore trade.

In the mid-1800s the predominant vessel on the lakes was the sailing ship, usually a small schooner. They visited every port and handled almost every type of cargo, including iron ore. At first they carried ore on deck, though later, as tonnages grew, it was placed in the cargo hold. Unfortunately, the sailing ship was a less than ideal ore carrier because its masts and rigging hindered dock operations at both ends of the lake.

Contemporary steamboats were less inclined to take on a cargo of iron ore, their interest was in hauling passengers or package freight. Moreover, because they used gangways to get their cargo into the hold there was no easy way to load iron ore. Given the need to move ore and the existing boats' impracticality for such service, it was decided to construct a boat specifically designed for the iron ore trade. Thus the first bulk freighter was born.

In 1869 the *R. J. HACKETT* was launched in Cleveland to carry iron ore. With an overall length of 211 feet and a 33 foot beam (width) she was a large boat for her day. Like all contemporary boats, the *HACKETT* was of all-wood construction, though in appearance she was like nothing previously seen on the lakes.

The *HACKETT* was patterned after small canal barges which were used to handle grain and other bulk cargoes. They were thus an ideal model for the *HACKETT's* builders to copy. The design was very straightforward and fundamental: simply place a large cargo hold between cabins at each end, one for the horses or mules hauling the tow rope and the other for the crew.

The *HACKETT* was similar in many respects, though much bigger. Also, she had a lake boat's hull which was better suited for service on the open lake. At the forward end was the pilot house and quarters for the deck crew while back aft were quarters for the galley crew and engine room personnel. In between was a large, spacious hold able to accommodate about 1,200 tons of iron ore. However, instead of horses or mules the *HACKETT* was steam-propelled, though perhaps as a gesture toward conservatism she also had masts fitted with sails.

Because of their heritage, and appearance, this type of boat was known as a "steambarge" rather than a "propeller" (which they had). Obviously this was meant to segregate them from other boats, perhaps some veteran lakemen looked down on such awkward looking craft. It wasn't until the 1890s that the term "steambarge" fell out of favor (as did "propeller".) By then all steam-powered vessels were simply being called "steamships."

Many of these early bulk freighters towed a barge to increase the amount of iron handled per trip. Sometimes new barges were built, though often an old sailing ship ended her days in such service. This practice too fell out of favor about 1900.

Dozens of new steambarges followed the *HACKETT* down the shipbuilders' ways in the years that followed. As with every new concept the design gradually evolved. One of the most obvious changes was the ever-increasing length. Another was the elimination of the sailing rig which was rarely used and only served to get in the way when at a dock.

In 1874 the *V. H. KETCHUM* was launched. With a 233 foot length and 41 foot beam, she was the largest boat on the Great Lakes. Though she was originally considered too big and perhaps even the maximum size that could see service on the lakes, other boats later surpassed her in length. She was indicative of the desire to increase the capacity of the ore fleet.

In the late 1880s and into the 1890s a new type of bulk freighter made an appearance, the "whaleback." Whalebacks, also known as "pigboats" because of their odd bow, offered some advantages when new, but they never found much favor in the industry and had no lasting influence on bulk freighter design.

The true limiting factor in boat length in the late 1800s was the draft (depth) in the rivers and harbors and the size of the locks at the Soo. For many years a 14-foot draft was common on the lakes, but by 1884 a 16-foot channel was standard and soon after pressure grew for a 20-foot channel. Accompanying the increased draft came the completion of the new Poe lock which was 800 feet long, 100 feet wide and 22 feet deep. This gave the designers an opportunity to dramatically increase the size of the new lakers entering service.

Another reason this became feasible was the adoption of steel construction. After the *SPOKANE* of 1886 proved herself practical, over the concerns of many experts who felt boats couldn't be built of steel, dozens of new steel lakers were put into service. The following table summarizes the growth in boat size, note particularly the jump from 1895 to 1906:

YEAR	BOAT NAME	LENGTH x BEAM
1869	R. J. HACKETT	211 ft. x 33 ft.
1874	V. H. KETCHUM	233 ft. x 41 ft.
1882	ONOKO (first iron boat)	287 ft. x 38 ft.
1886	SPOKANE (first steel boat)	310 ft. x 38 ft.
1895	VICTORY	400 ft. x 48 ft.
1900	ISSAC L. ELLWOOD	498 ft. x 52 ft.
1904	AUGUSTUS B. WOLVIN	560 ft. x 56 ft.
1906	J. PIERPONT MORGAN	605 ft. x 58 ft.
1943	SEWELL AVERY	620 ft. x 60 ft.
1951	JOSEPH H. THOMPSON	715 ft. x 71.4 ft.
1960	ARTHUR B. HOMER	730 ft. x 75 ft.
1972	ROGER BLOUGH	858 ft. x 105 ft.
1972	STUART J. CORT	1,000 ft. x 105 ft.
1981	WILLIAM J. DeLANCEY	1,013 ft. x 105 ft.

Note: this list is only intended to be representative of boat sizes and doesn't necessarily indicate the first boat of a given length.

Of the boats noted above, it was perhaps the *AUGUSTUS B. WOLVIN* of 1904 that was one of the most significant. She did away with the usual deck beams and stanchions in the cargo hold and instead used a large arch to form one large hold. This was easier to load and unload and eliminated much of the hand work needed to trim or clean up the hold at either end of the lakes. By 1905 almost all new lakers were built to this design and many older boats were reconstructed.

Other changes were adopted over the years on the lakers: the enclosed pilot house about 1908, radio direction finders, tunnels, etc. However, these were more evolutionary than revolutionary in nature so there was little change from the basic design. After 1910, the 600-foot boat was considered "standard" so dozens were built in the years that followed.

A typical 600-foot boat had a beam of about 60 feet and carried about 12,500 tons of ore per trip. It should be noted that iron ore is referred to in "gross" tons of 2,240 pounds within the industry. Each boat could make a round trip about every seven days between Duluth and the lower lake ports during a season that ran from mid-April to late November.

In 1908 the *WYANDOTTE* was built in Detroit. She was similar to conventional bulk freighters except for self-unloading equipment consisting of hoppers in the cargo hold, conveyor belts, and a boom for placing cargo on the dock. Self-unloaders soon became a common sight on the lakes, though they usually carried coal, stone, or cargoes other than iron ore, the older "straight deck" bulkers continued to dominate that trade.

About 1981 the original straight-decker was finally replaced by self-unloaders in the ore trade. All new boats in the American fleet and many Canadians were being built as self-unloaders and most ore docks were now able to accomodate them. As a result many of the newer straight-deckers were either converted to self-unloaders or were scrapped. Today it's the era of the self-unloader and sights like those on many of the pages that follow are gone forever.

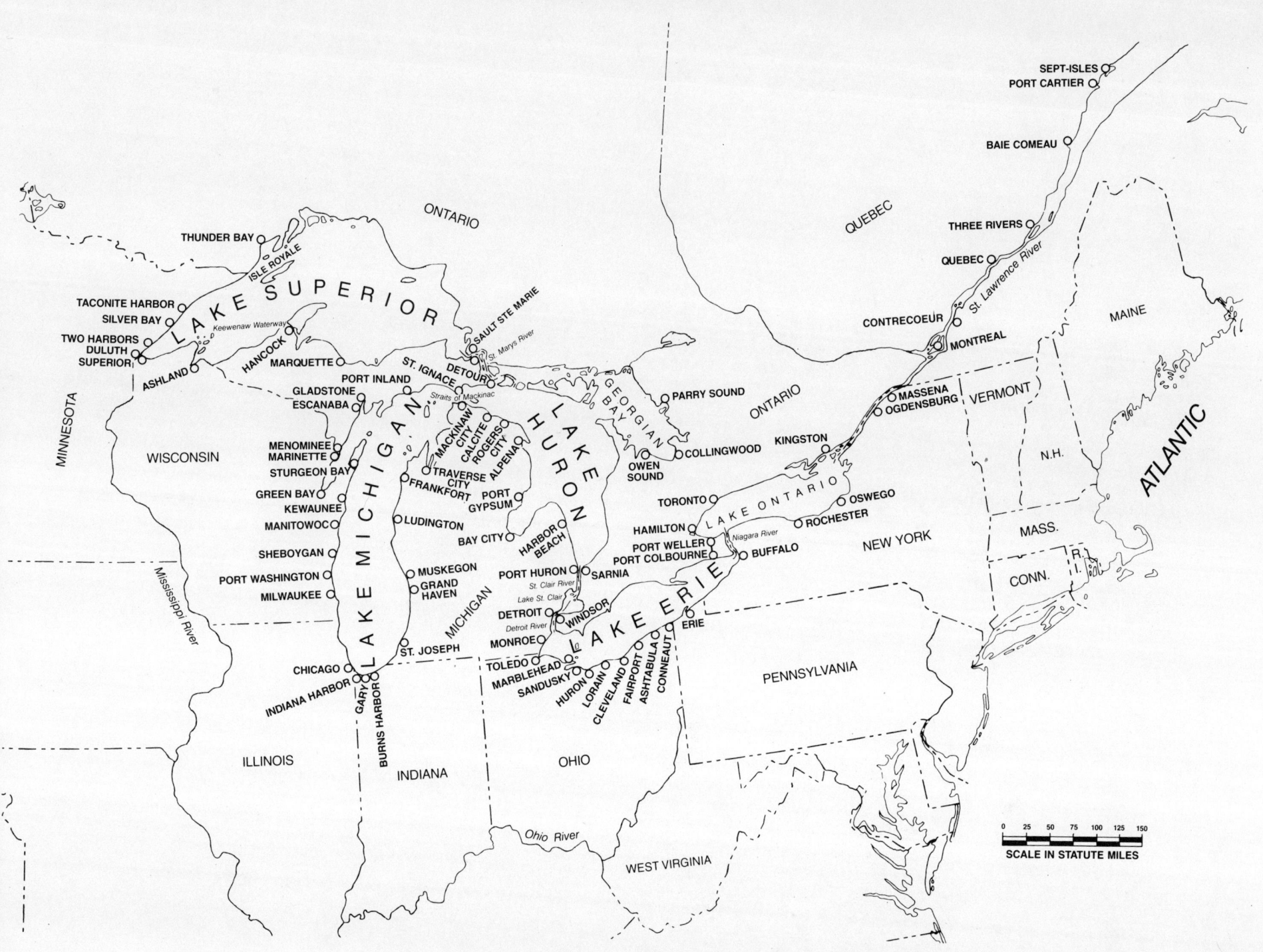

Listed below is a typical caption for one of the boats in this book:

33 **E. M. FORD** 413'-9" x 50'-0" x 28'-0" Cleveland Shipbuilding Company, Cleveland, OH May 25, 1898 Hull # 30 Presque Isle 1898-1956 **E. M. FORD** **1956-** Cleveland-Cliffs SS Company 1898-1956 **HURON PORTLAND CEMENT CO.** **1956-1987** Chrysler Leasing Inc. (Inland Lakes) 1987- Upbound at the Sugar Island ferry crossing in October 1958 with the old Huron fleet green hull, since replaced by grey. *William D. Carle III.*	This entry can be deciphered as follows: *33* - page number of the photograph ***E. M. FORD*** - name of the boat depicted *413'-9" x 50'-0" x 28'-0"* - registered dimensions of boat: length between perpendiculars, beam, depth *Cleveland Shipbuilding Company* - builder *Cleveland, OH* - place built *May 25, 1898* - date launched *Hull # 30* - builder's hull number *Presque Isle* - former (or subsequent) name *1898-1956* - years above name was used ***E. M. FORD*** - name of boat when photographed *Cleveland-Cliffs SS Co.* - previous (or subsequent) owner* ***HURON PORTLAND CEMENT CO.*** - owner when photograph was taken.* *Upbound . . .* - caption detailing when and where photograph was taken. *William D. Carle III.* - photographer

*In many cases the owner does not operate the boat but hires a vessel manager. In these cases, the name of the agent or managing fleet is shown thus:

Pioneer Shipping, Ltd. (Misener)   1980-

  In this case the boat has been owned by Pioneer Shipping but operated by the Misener fleet since 1980.
  Many familiar names will be found in these listings, names like Oakes, Hutchinson, etc. It's also interesting to note how many boats changed fleets over the years as well as names.

9
SILVER ISLE
713'-9" x 75'-3" x 35'-5"
Verelme Ship Yard, Cork, Ireland
November 23, 1962   Hull # 662

SILVER ISLE	**1962-**
Mohawk Navigation Co., Ltd.	1962-1970
Mohawk Navigation Co., Ltd. (Misener)	1970-1980
PIONEER SHIPPING, LTD. (MISENER)	**1980-**

The SILVER ISLE is passing through the Welland on a May 1986 day. The Pioneer ships are undoubtedly the most colorful lakers around! *Jim Semon.*

10
B. F. JONES
520'-0" x 54'-0" x 26'-2"
West Bay City Shipbuilding Co., W. Bay City, MI
November 29, 1906   Hull # 621

General Garretson	1907-1935
E. J. Kulas	1935-1936
Powhatan	1936-1937
Charles A. Paul	1937-1956
B. F. JONES	**1956-1973**
Gilchrist Transportation Co.	1907-1913
Wilson Marine Transit Co.	1913-1967
Ingalls Shpbldg Corp. (Wilson)	1967-1968
LITTON SYSTEMS, INC. (WILSON)	**1968-1973**
Kinsman Marine Transit Co.	1973
	Sold/scrap

In Whitefish Bay in July 1969. A typical, yet classic pose of a laker underway. For many years Wilson's white "W" on a black stack was a familiar sight on the Great Lakes. *Eric Hirsimaki.*

11
THE WINTER RUN

It's winter, but the boats are still running. In this scene the EDGAR B. SPEER arrives in Duluth covered with ice after a trip across the frigid Lake Superior waters. The ice and mist serve to remind us of what it's like on the big lake — even in summer. *Tim Slattery.*

12
SEAWAY QUEEN
717'-3" x 76'-2" x 25'-5"
Port Weller Drydock, Ltd., Port Weller, ONT
1959   Hull # 25

SEAWAY QUEEN	**1959-**
UPPER LAKES SHIPPING, LTD.	**1959-**

The SEAWAY QUEEN was one of the first large boats built in Canada after the completion of the St. Lawrence Seaway. She has been used extensively during her career in the ore and grain trades. *Dave Lawler* captured this view of her in June 1977.

13
CHARLES E. WILSON
666'-8" x 78'-1" x 42'-7"
Bay Shipbuilding Corporation, Sturgeon Bay, WI
March 10, 1973   Hull # 710

CHARLES E. WILSON	**1973-**
FRANKLIN SS CO. (B&C)	**1973-1978**
American SS Co.	1978-

The WILSON unloads at the stone dock in Huron, Ohio in August 1975. *Eric Hirsimaki.*

14
RHODE ISLAND
78'-8" x 20'-0" x 12'-4"
Great Lakes Towing Company, Cleveland, OH
7-13-30   Hull # 65

RHODE ISLAND	**1930-**
GREAT LAKES TOWING COMPANY	**1930-**

Converted from steam to diesel in 1958.

Much of a tug's time is spent hurrying to or from a tow. This particular view of the RHODE ISLAND in Duluth Harbor shows that even when the tug isn't on a towline it can be an interesting boat to watch. *Tim Slattery.*

15
CHARLES M. SCHWAB
658'-3" x 60'-2" x 28'-0"
American Shipbuilding Company, Cleveland, OH
June 19, 1923   Hull # 496

CHARLES M. SCHWAB	**1923-1975**
Pierson Daughters	1975-1982
Beechglen	1982-
Interlake SS Co.	1923-1966
Pickands Mather & Co.	1966-1973
INTERLAKE SS CO.	**1973-1975**
Robert Pierson Holdings	1975-1982
P&H Shipping Co.	1982-

Lengthened 72'-0" in 1960 and stern from tanker GULFPORT added in place of original.

Arriving in Huron, Ohio on a November 1973 day. *Jim Semon.*

16
THE CLEVELANDER
58'-4" x 16'-0" x 6'-4"
Paasch Marine Service, Erie, PA
1954   Hull #

THE CLEVELANDER	**1954-1980**
CITY OF CLEVELAND, OHIO	**1954-1974**
Marine Development Co.	1974-1980
	Sold

Converted to tug in 1974. Sold to British buyers and sent to Europe.

THE CLEVELANDER's role is aptly demonstrated by her crew in this circa 1962 view. *Bruce Dicken.*

17
COLLISION BEND

This June 1975 scene shows the THOMAS W. LAMONT working her way up the Cuyahoga River to the Central Furnace dock in Cleveland. The location is known as "Collision Bend" due to the fact that bowsprits of sailing vessels often snagged one another here in days long past. *David Lawler.*

18
UNGAVA TRANSPORT
403′-4″ x 55′-5″ x 21′-2″
Sarpsborg M/V A/S, Greaker, Norway
November 11, 1958   Hull # 30

Varangnes	1959-1970
Tommy Wilborg	1970-1974
UNGAVA TRANSPORT	**1974-1985**
Sameiet Varangskip II	1959-1970
K/S A/S Geir & Co. III	1970-1974
HALL CORPORATION SHIPPING, LTD.	**1974-1985**
	Sold/scrap

Converted from ore/oil carrier to tanker in 1971.

In the Welland Canal in August 1979. *Jim Bartke.*

19
NORISLE
203′-3″ x 36′-1″ x 14′-9″
Collingwood Shipyard, Ltd., Collingwood, ONT
October 17, 1946   Hull # 136

NORISLE	**1946-1985**
DOMINION & OWEN SOUND TRANS. CO., LTD.	**1946-1985**
	Sold*

* Sold to Township of Assignash, ONT. On display at Maitowanig, ONT.

In Georgian Bay in June 1971. *Christine Rohn Hilston.*

20
WILLIAM A. WHITNEY
100′-0″ x 24′-1″ x 11′-2″
Whitney Brothers, Superior, WI
May 5, 1920   Hull # 61

WILLIAM A. WHITNEY	**1920-**
Whitney Bros Co.	1920-1931
Merritt, Chapman & Scott Co.	1931-1963
Zenith Dredge Co.	1963-1975
TUG KILLARNEY, INC. (GAELIC)	**1975-**

The WHITNEY at Detroit in April 1982. She's one of the classic tugs on the lakes and is often used to break ice. *Eric Hirsimaki.*

21
LAKEWOOD
377′-0″ x 48′-2″ x 24′-0″
Chicago Shipbuilding Company, Chicago, IL
April 25, 1903   Hull # 58

Charles M. Warner	1903-1928
Michigan	1928-1956
LAKEWOOD	**1956-**
U.S. Transportation Company	1903-1911
Great Lakes SS Company	1911-1928
Great Lakes Dredge & Dock Company	1928-1956
Presque Isle Trans. Co. (Erie Sand)	1956-1969
ERIE SAND SS COMPANY	**1969-**

Built as bulk freighter, converted to sand dredge in 1928. Converted to self-unloader in 1957.

A familiar sight around Cleveland, the LAKEWOOD is winding her way up the Cuyahoga to unload another cargo of sand in June 1978. *Eric Hirsimaki.*

22
ALBERT E. HEEKIN
525′-0″ x 58′-0″ x 31′-0″
American Shipbuilding Company, Lorain, OH
September 15, 1917   Hull # 723

William A. Amberg	1917-1932
ALBERT E. HEEKIN	**1932-1955**
Silver Bay	1955-1975
Judith M. Pierson	1975-1982
Fernglen	1982-1984
Producers SS Co. (Hanna)	1917-1936
NATIONAL STEEL CORP. (HANNA)	**1936-1955***
Wilson Marine Transit Co.	1955-1957
Republic Steel Corp. (Wilson)	1957-1971
Kinsman Transit Co.	1971-1975
R. Pierson Holdings (Soo River)	1975-1977
Pierson SS Co. (Soo River)	1977-1982
P&H Shipping, Ltd.	1982-1984
	Sold/scrap

* In 1955 the HEEKIN and the Louis W. Hill were traded to Wilson for the Ben Moreell.

The HEEKIN is shown at Huron, Ohio under the old steam-hydraulic unloaders about 1948. *Eric Hirsimaki Collection.*

23
MERCURY
373′-0″ x 52′-0″ x 25′-0″
American Shipbuilding Company, Lorain, OH
May 20, 1911   Hull # 396

Renown	1912-1930
Beaumont Parks	1930-1957
MERCURY	**1957-1975**
Derrick No. 3	1980*-
Standard Oil Co.	1912-1957
CLEVELAND TANKERS	**1957-1975**
Roen Salvage Co.	1980*-

* Sold for scrap in 1975 and partially cut up before conversion to a barge.

Downbound in the St. Clair River in August 1969. *Eric Hirsimaki.*

24
HENRY LaLIBERTE
530′-0″ x 56′-2″ x 32′-0″
Great Lakes Engineering Works, Ecorse, MI
May 16, 1908   # 42

James Corrigan	1908-1916
Arthur E. Newbold	1916-1925
Maryland	1925-1954
HENRY LaLIBERTE	**1954-1974**
Frontier SS Co. (Mills)	1908-1916
Johnstown SS Co. (Hanna)	1916-1925
Bethlehem Transportation Co.	1925-1954
BUCKEYE SS CO. (HUTCHINSON)	**1954-1969**
Kinsman Marine Transit Co.	1969-1974
	Sold/scrap

Upbound in the St. Marys River, September 1961. *William D. Carle III.*

25
SUNRISE IN DULUTH

What was once a common scene, a traditional laker entering Duluth Harbor, has become a rarity in the late 1980s. A colorful early morning sunrise imparts a mood to this picture that does full justice to this visage of another era. *Tim Slattery.*

26
L. E. BLOCK
604'-2" x 64'-2" x 28'-6"
American Shipbuilding Co., Lorain, OH
February 1, 1927   Hull # 795

L. E. BLOCK	**1927-1986**
Inland Steel Co. (Hutchinson)	1927-1957
INLAND STEEL CO.	**1957-1986**
Escanaba Basic Marine	1986-

The BLOCK works her way upriver on a rare visit to Cleveland in June 1978. *Eric Hirsimaki.*

27
WILLIAM J. DeLANCEY
1000'-0" x 105'-0" x 56'-0"
American Shipbuilding Co., Lorain, OH
April 25, 1981   Hull # 909

WILLIAM J. DeLANCEY	**1981-**
INTERLAKE SS CO. (PM)	**1981-1986**
Interlake SS Co.	1986-

The DeLANCEY leaves Lorain, Ohio for her sea trials. *Mel Schurdell.*

28
JOAN M. McCULLOUGH
586'-3" x 60'-2" x 27'-9"
American Shipbuilding Co., Lorain, OH
October 7, 1926   Hull # 793

William McLauchlan	1926-1966
Samuel Mather	1966-1975
JOAN M. McCULLOUGH	**1975-1982**
Birchglen	1982-
Interlake SS Co.	1926-1966
Pickands Mather & Co.	1966-1973
Interlake SS Co.	1973-1975
ROBERT PIERSON HOLDINGS, LTD. (SOO R.)	**1975-1977**
Pierson Steamships, Ltd. (Soo River)	1977-1982
P&H Shipping, Ltd.	1982-

The McCULLOUGH still carries some of her PM paint in this picture taken during the early part of her Soo River career. She's departing Huron, Ohio in April 1975. *Jim Semon.*

29
ERIE QUEEN
139'-5" x 30'-0" x 14'-1"
Rice Brothers Corp., E. Boothbay, ME
1922   Hull #

Bainbridge	1922-1936
Algomah II	1936-1962
ERIE QUEEN	**1962-1969**
Benton Transit Co.	1922-1926
Vern Beckwith-Trustee (Benton)	1926-1928
Farmers & Merchants Bank (Benton)	1928-1930
Farmers & Merchants Bank (Goodrich)	1930-1934
Maritime Securities Co.	1934-1935
James F. Keightly (Inland Trans.)	1935-1937
Edith M. Keightly (Inland Trans.)	1937-1947
Arnold Transit Co.	1947-1962
WASAC WATERWAYS, INC.	**1962-1966**
Acme Scrap Iron & Metal	1966-1968
Pier Restaurant, Inc.	1968-1969
	Sold*

Laid down as trawler ARNOLD T. RICE, but completed as a passenger ferry.

The ERIE QUEEN is tied up in the Cuyahoga River in Cleveland about 1962. *Bruce Dicken.*

30
WILLIS B. BOYER
590'-0" x 64'-2" x 34'-2"
Great Lakes Engineering Works, Ecorse, MI
July 1, 1911   Hull # 82

Col. James M. Schoonmaker	1911-1969
WILLIS B. BOYER	**1969-1987**
Shenango Furnace Co.	1911-1969
INTERLAKE SS CO.*	**1969-1971**
Cleveland-Cliffs SS Co.	1971-1983
American Bulk Shipping	1983-1986
Cleveland-Cliffs SS Co.	1986
	Sold**

* Leased to Republic Steel Corp. during 1969-1971.
** Sold to the City of Toledo, Ohio for display.

Upbound in the St. Marys River in September 1971. *William D. Carle III.*

31
LEHIGH
603'-8" x 60'-2" x 30'-2"
Great Lakes Engineering Works, River Rouge, MI
July 24, 1943   Hull # 295

Mesabi	1943
LEHIGH	**1943-1981**
Joseph X. Robert	1981-1982
Willowglen	1982-
U.S. Maritime Commission	1943
BETHLEHEM STEEL CORP.	**1943-1981**
Pierson SS's, Ltd.	1981-1982
P&H Shipping, Ltd.	1982-

Upbound in the St. Marys River in September 1972. *William D. Carle III.*

32
FRONTENAC
709'-3" x 75'-0" x 39'-7"
Davie Shipbuilding, Ltd., Levis, QUE
December 12, 1967   Hull # 661

FRONTENAC	**1967-**
CANADA SS LINES INC.	**1967-1976**
Power Corp. of Canada, Ltd. (CSL)	1976-

Converted to a self-unloader in 1973.

Upbound in the Detroit River in August 1969. *Eric Hirsimaki.*

33
E. M. FORD
406'-0" x 50'-0" x 28'-0"
Cleveland Shipbuilding Co., Cleveland, OH
May 25, 1898   Hull # 30

Presque Isle	1898-1956
E. M. FORD	**1956-**
Cleveland-Cliffs SS Co.	1898-1956
HURON PORTLAND CEMENT CO.	**1956-1987**
Chrysler Leasing, Inc. (Inland Lakes)	1987-

Upbound at the Sugar Island ferry crossing in October 1958. Note the green hull, since replaced by grey. *William D. Carle III.*

34 BROOKDALE
509'-7" x 54'-2" x 26'-7"
American Shipbuilding Company, Lorain, OH
July 31, 1909   Hull # 371

J. S. Ashley	1909-1962
Fred A. Manske	1962-1976
BROOKDALE	**1976-1980**
Kinney SS Co.	1909-1936
Pioneer SS Co. (Hutchinson)	1936-1961
American SS Co. (B&C)	1961-1976
DALE TRANSPORTS, LTD. (WESTDALE)	**1976-1980**
	Sold/scrap

Converted to self-unloader in 1936.

Passing under Cuyahoga River Bridge #1 in Cleveland in September 1977. *Jim Semon.*

35 CHIEF WAWATAM
338'-8" x 62'-0" x 20'-7"
Toledo Shipbuilding Company, Toledo, OH
August 26, 1911   Hull # 119

CHIEF WAWATAM	**1911-**
Mackinac Transportation Co.	1911-1977
STATE OF MICHIGAN (STRAITS CARFERRY)	**1977-**

The CHIEF was often used as an ice breaker in the Straits of Mackinac area. She's shown here pushing thru ice on a April 1977 day. *G. W. Deucher.*

36 DULUTH HARBOR

Duluth-Superior Harbor has always been a busy place. In this August 1980 scene, the WALTER A. STERLING is passing thru the Wisconsin Draw while CSL and PM boats load at the Duluth, Missabe & Iron Range RR ore docks. In the foreground is a loaded ore train that has just come down the hill from Proctor. Because of the steep grade it's shrouded by brakeshoe smoke. In the distance can be seen the Burlington Nortern's ore docks in Superior, Wisconsin. Four laid up U.S. Steel boats strike a discordant note. A typical picture of Duluth Harbor. *Eric Hirsimaki.*

37 HELEN EVANS
538'-4" x 56'-2" x 27'-3"
Great Lakes Engineering Works, Ecorse, MI
April 7, 1907   Hull # 16

James Laughlin	1906-1964
HELEN EVANS	**1964-1980**
Interstate SS Co. (Hayden)	1906-1909
Interstate SS Co. (Becker)	1909-1920
Interstate SS Co. (England)	1920-1943
Interstate SS Co. (Tietjen)	1943-1949
Jones & Laughlin Steel Corp.	1949-1952
Wilson Marine Transit Co.	1952-1964
HINDMAN TRANSPORTATION CO., LTD.	**1964-1978**
Quebec & Ontario Trans. Co., Ltd.	1978-1980
	Sold/scrap

The HELEN EVENS clears Huron, Ohio late on a September 1977 day. *Jim Semon.*

38 SENATOR OF CANADA
604'-9" x 62'-0" x 33'-0"
Canadian Shpbldg and Engrg, Ltd., Collingwood, ONT
May 30, 1957   Hull # 159

SENATOR OF CANADA	**1957-1985**
N. M. PATERSON & SONS, LTD.	**1957-1985**
	Sold/scrap

Passing through the Welland Canal in September 1978. *Mel Schurdell.*

39 WILLIAM R. ROESCH
612'-1± x 68'-2± x 34'-4±
American Shipbuilding Company, Lorain, OH
June 22, 1973   Hull # 901

WILLIAM R. ROESCH	**1973-**
UNION COMMERCE BANK (KINSMAN)	**1973-1976**
Union Commerce Bank (Pringle)	1976-

The ROESCH is entering the Cuyahoga River at Cleveland in October 1974. They must be painting the after house since it's covered with red lead. *Dave Lawler.*

40 ALPENA
356'-0" x 47'-2" x 27'-0"
Detroit Shipbuilding Co., Wyandotte, MI
March 24, 1909   Hull # 177

ALPENA	**1909-1968**
Sidney E. Smith, Jr.	1968-1972
Alpena	1972
Wyandotte Trans. Co.	1909-1965
Erie Sand & Gravel Co. (Columbia)	1965-1966
ERIE MOTORSHIP CO. (ERIE SAND)	**1966-1969**
Erie Sand SS Co.	1969-1972
	Sold/scrap

Arriving at the sand dock in Ashtabula in October 1967. *Eric Hirsimaki.*

41 ASHLAND
603'-8" x 60'-2" x 30'-2"
Great Lakes Engineering Works, Ashtabula, OH
December 19, 1942   Hull # 523

Clarence B. Randall	1943-1962
ASHLAND	**1962-**
Pioneer SS Co. (Hutchinson)	1943-1962
OGLEBAY NORTON COMPANY (COLUMBIA)	**1962-**

Upbound near Detour, August 1968. *Eric Hirsimaki.*

42 FORT YORK
445'-7" x 56'-2" x 28'-2"
Collingwood Shipyard, Ltd., Collingwood, ONT
January 15, 1958   Hull # 158

FORT YORK	**1958-1985**
unknown barge	1985-
Canada SS Lines, Ltd.	1958-1976
POWER CORP. OF CANADA, LTD. (CSL)	**1976-1985**
Charpat Trans., Inc.	1985-

Cut down to a barge in 1985.

The FORT YORK eases out of lock #3 at the Soo in June 1977. *Dave Lawler.*

43 — MATTHEW ANDREWS
602'-8" x 64'-2" x 28'-5"
Great Lakes Engineering Works, River Rouge, MI
October, 1924   Hull # 247

Edward J. Berwind	1924-1963
MATTHEW ANDREWS	**1963-1974**
Blanche Hindman	1974-1979
Lac Ste. Anne	1979-1985
Franklin SS. Co. (Oakes)	1924-1930
Franklin SS. Co. (Bethlehem)	1930-1941
Franklin SS. Co. (Hanna)	1941-1943
Hanna Ore Company	1943-1945
Hanna Coal and Ore Corporation	1945-1959
HANNA MINING CO.	**1959-1974**
Hindman Transportation Co., Ltd.	1974-1978
Quebec & Ontario Trans. Co., Ltd.	1978-1984
Transport Desgagnes, Inc.	1984-1985
	Sold/scrap

The ANDREWS arrives at Huron, Ohio in July 1967. *Charles Matt/Jim Semon Collection.*

44 — EDWARD L. RYERSON
712'-0" x 75'-0" x 39'-0"
Manitowoc Shipbuilding, Inc., Manitowoc, WI
1960   Hull # 425

EDWARD L. RYERSON	**1960-**
INLAND STEEL CO.	**1960-**

Downbound near DeTour in August 1969. *Eric Hirsimaki.*

45 — ELMDALE
444'-0" x 56'-2" x 28'-0"
Great Lakes Engineering Works, Ecorse, MI
January 30, 1909   Hull # 56

Clifford F. Moll	1909-1933
Standard Portland Cement	1933-1960
ELMDALE	**1960-1979**
American SS Company (B&C)	1909-1960
REDWOOD ENTERPRISES, LTD.	**1960-1979**
	Sold/scrap

Upbound at the mouth of the Detroit River in August 1969. *Eric Hirsimaki.*

46-47 — ALGOWEST
730'-0" x 75'-6" x 26'-6"
Canadian Shipbldg and Engrg Co., Collingwood, ONT
April 16, 1982   Hull # 226

ALGOWEST	**1982-**
ALGOMA CENTRAL RAILWAY	**1982-**

Approaching Detroit in September 1982. *Eric Hirsimaki.*

48 — ELTON HOYT 2ND
683'-0" x 70'-0" x 37'-0"
Beth.-Sparrows Pt. Shpyd, Inc., Sparrows Pt., MD
March 3, 1952   Hull # 4512

ELTON HOYT 2ND	**1952-**
Interlake SS Co. (PM)	1952-1966
Pickands Mather & Co.	1966-1973
INTERLAKE SS CO. (PM)	**1973-1986**
Interlake SS Co.	1986-

Lengthened 72'-0" in 1957. Converted to self-unloader in 1980.

Arriving in Huron, Ohio in July 1975. *Eric Hirsimaki.*

49 — GEORGE STEPHENSON
407'-4" x 49'-0" x 23'-4"
F. W. Wheeler & Co., W. Bay City, MI
September 23, 1896   Hull # 116

GEORGE STEPHENSON	**1896-1963**
Bessemer SS Co.	1896-1901
Pittsburgh SS Co.	1901-1939
BUCKEYE SS CO. (HUTCHINSON)	**1939-1959**
Beta Lake Ship Co. (Continental Grain)	1959-1963
Diesel Sales and Service, Ltd.	1963
	Scrapped

Converted to a barge in 1959.

The STEPHENSON and her consort, the barge MAGNA, are upbound in the St. Marys River in October 1958. *William D. Carle III.*

50 — EDWARD B. GREENE
749'-4" x 70'-2" x 31'-3"
American Shipbuilding Company, Toledo, OH
January 10, 1952   Hull # 189

EDWARD B. GREENE	**1952-1985**
Benson Ford	1985-
CLEVELAND-CLIFFS SS CO.	**1952-1985**
Rouge Steel Company	1985-

Lengthened 120'-0" in 1976. Converted to self-unloader in 1981.

The GREENE is shown arriving at Ashtabula, Ohio in June 1978. *Mel Schurdell.*

51 — SHARON
656'-0" x 68'-2" x 39'-2"
Alabama Drydock and Shipbuilding Co., Mobile, AL
1945   Hull # 346

Archers Hope	1947-1957
Joseph S. Young	1957-1969
H. Lee White	1969-1974
SHARON	**1974-1986**
U.S. Maritime Commission	1945-1948
Ships, Inc.	1948-1956
AMERICAN SS CO. (B&C)	**1956-1986**
	Sold/scrap

Built as a tanker. Lengthened 69'-0" and converted to self-unloader in 1957. Lengthened an additional 84'-0" in 1966.

At the stone dock in Huron, Ohio. May 1977. *Jim Semon.*

52 — WOLVERINE
610'-0" x 68'-0" x 36'-11"
American Shipbuilding Company, Lorain, OH
September 9, 1974   Hull # 903

WOLVERINE	**1974-**
OGLEBAY NORTON CO. (COLUMBIA)	**1974-**

Downbound in the Detroit River in September 1982. *Eric Hirsimaki.*

53   GEORGE HINDMAN
623'-2" x 67'-2" x 30'-4"
Canadian Shipbldg and Engrng, Ltd., Midland, ONT
October 15, 1949   Hull # 34

Coverdale	1949-1973
GEORGE HINDMAN	**1973-1979**
Meldrum Bay	1979-1985
Canada Steamship Lines, Ltd.	1949-1961
Ocean Lines, Ltd. (CSL)	1961-1971
Pipe Line Tankers, Ltd. (CSL)	1971-1973
HINDMAN TRANSPORTATION CO., LTD.	**1973-1979**
Quebec & Ontario Trans. Co., Ltd.	1979-1985
Upper Lakes Shipping, Ltd.	1985
	Sold/scrap

Downbound in the lower St. Mary's River in June 1977. *David Lawler.*

54   L'ORME #1
415'-0" x 60'-0" x 29'-0"
Marine Industries, Ltd., Sorel, QUE
August 24, 1974   Hull # 413

Leon Simard	1974-1981
L'ORME #1	**1981-**
Branch Lines, Ltd.	1974-1979
Davie Shipbuilding, Ltd.	1979-1982
SOCONAV	**1982-**

At Three Rivers, Quebec. June 1983. *Jim Bartke.*

55   RALPH H. WATSON
593'-3" x 60'-2" x 28'-2"
Great Lakes Engineering Works, River Rouge, MI
November 20, 1937   Hull # 285

RALPH H. WATSON	**1937-1986**
Pittsburgh Steamship Co.	1937-1952
U.S. STEEL CORP.	**1952-1981**
USS Great Lakes Fleet, Inc.	1981-1986
	Sold/scrap

Downbound at the Soo Locks in September 1966. *Eric Hirsimaki.*

56   G. A. TOMLINSON
532'-0" x 58'-2" x 32'-0"
Great Lakes Engineering Works, Ecorse, MI
March 12, 1907   Hull # 29

D. O. Mills	1907-1960
G. A. TOMLINSON	**1960-1980**
Interlake SS Co.	1907-1959
Tomlinson Fleet Corp.	1959-1971
COLUMBIA TRANSPORTATION CO.	**1971-1979**
	Sold/scrap

Dumping stone in Cleveland Harbor for a new diked disposal area, June 1978. *Robert Todten.*

57   BAYTON
416'-0" x 50'-0" x 28'-0"
American Shipbuilding Company, Cleveland, OH
April 7, 1904   Hull # 421

Francis Widlar	1904-1921
BAYTON	**1921-1966**
Columbia SS Co. (Becker)	1904-1916
Interstate SS Co. (Becker)	1916-1920
William H. Becker	1920-1921
Matthews SS's, Ltd.	1921-1932
Frederick C. Clarkson	1932-1933
Colonial SS's, Ltd.	1933-1960
SCOTT MISENER STEAMSHIPS, LTD.	**1960-1966**
	Sold/scrap

Downbound in the St. Marys River in October 1965. *Charles Matt/Jim Semon Collection.*

58   DES GROSEILLIERS
269'-0" x 64'-0" x 32'-0"
Port Weller Drydocks, Ltd., Port Weller, ONT
February 20, 1982   Hull # 68

DES GROSEILLIERS	**1982-**
CANADIAN MINISTRY OF TRANSPORT	**1982-**

The sun's first rays find the DES GROSEILLIERS at her berth in Quebec. Unfortunately, except for photographer *Dave Lawler* and those standing watch few witnessed this impressive June 1982 scene.

59   WILTRANCO I
535'-8" x 60'-0" x 27'-0"
Toledo Shipbuilding Company, Toledo, OH
April 17, 1917   Hull # 137

Horace S. Wilkinson	1917-1963
WILTRANCO I	**1963-1973**
Great Lakes SS Co.	1917-1957
Wilson Marine Transit	1957-1967
Ingalls S/B Corp. (Wilson)	1967-1969
CLYDE VAN ENKEVORT	**1969-1973**
(ESCANABA TOWING)	
Industrial Fuel & Asphalt Co.	1973
	Sold/scrap

Upbound in the St. Marys River in September 1972. *William D. Carle III.*

60-61   JOSEPH H. THOMPSON
696'-0" x 71'-7" x 25'-6"
Sun Shipbuilding & Drydock Co., Chester, PA
1944   Hull # 342

Marine Robin	1944-1950
JOSEPH H. THOMPSON	**1950-**
U.S. Maritime Commission	1944-1950
Wisconsin-Michigan SS Co.	1950
HANSAND SS CO. (HANNA)	**1950-1984**
Upper Lakes Towing Co.	1984-

Built as a troopship. Lengthened 199'-0" and converted to bulk carrier in 1952.

The THOMPSON loads red ore at the DM&IR dock in Duluth on Labor Day 1982. For the first run of ore into the cargo hold there's a chute for each hatch. *Eric Hirsimaki.*

62   ANCHORED FOR FOG

To the lake boats fog represents a hazard that must be taken seriously. On the open lake it's bad enough, but in the rivers it can shut down all operations because of the lack of visibility. A captain has to anchor and simply wait it out. In this view a P&H boat waits for the fog to clear in the St. Lawrence in November 1982. *Dave Lawler.*

63   CANADIAN PROSPECTOR
705'-5" x 75'-5" x 43'-2"
Short Bros., Ltd., Sunderland, England
October 17, 1963   Hull # 542

Carlton	1964-1975
Federal Wear	1975
St. Lawrence Prospector	1975-1979
CANADIAN PROSPECTOR	**1979-**
Chapman & Willam, Ltd.	1964-1975
Port Weller Drydocks, Ltd. (ULS)	1975-1979
Niagara Finance Corp., Ltd. (ULS)	1979-1981
CONTINENTAL BANK CAPITAL CORP. (ULS)	**1981-**

Lengthened 80'-0" in 1968 and 97'-0" in 1979.

At Port Weller, Ontario in June 1983. *Jim Bartke.*

64   UHLMAN BROTHERS
525'-0:dp x 5'-0" x 31'-0"
American Shipbuilding Company, Lorain, OH
February 10, 1906   Hull # 341

Loftus Cuddy	1906-1916
C. S. Robinson	1916-1965
UHLMAN BROTHERS	**1965-1973**
Cleveland SS Company (Mitchell)	1906-1915
Interlake SS Company (PM)	1915-1954
KINSMAN MARINE TRANSIT COMPANY	**1954-1973**
	Sold/scrap

Downbound at the Upper Piers at the Soo in August 1969. *Eric Hirsimaki.*

65   FOLLOW THE LEADER

The KINSMAN INDEPENDENT is helped up the Cuyahoga River by the tugs VERMONT and IOWA (out of sight behind the bow) in September 1985. By now it's rare to see a straight-decker at all and only the Kinsman boats and a few Canadians keep the species alive. The tugs will help the INDEPENDENT around the bend at Settlers Landing to the Cereal Foods dock where she'll unload her cargo of grain. On this crisp autumn day sights such as this are a joy to behold. *Eric Hirsimaki.*

66   SOUTH AMERICAN
290'-6" x 47'-1" x 18'-3"
Great Lakes Engineering Works, Ecorse, MI
1914   Hull # 133

SOUTH AMERICAN	**1914-1974**
CHICAGO, DULUTH & GEORGIAN BAY TRANSPORTATION CO.	**1914-1967**
Seamans International Union	1967-1974
	Sold/scrap

Her engines were removed and the boat converted to a training ship on the East Coast in 1967.

The SOUTH AMERICAN is in the Welland Canal on the occasion of her only passage up the Seaway. July 1967. *Charles Matt/Jim Semon Collection.*

67   COURTNEY BURTON
670'-3" x 70'-0" x 37'-0"
American Shipbuilding Co., Lorain, OH
November 19, 1952   Hull # 869

Ernest T. Weir	1952-1978
COURTNEY BURTON	**1978-**
National Steel Corp. (Hanna)	1952-1978
OGLEBAY NORTON COMPANY (COLUMBIA)	**1978-**

Converted to self-unloader in 1981.

Upbound in the St. Marys River in September 1979. *Mel Schurdell.*

68   CHICAGO TRIBUNE
253'-3" x 43'-9" x 23'-0"
Earle's Shipbldg & Engrg, Ltd., Hull, England
1930   Hull # 676

Thorold	1930-1933
CHICAGO TRIBUNE	**1933-1986**
QUEBEC & ONTARIO TRANS. CO., LTD.	**1933-1986**
Group Desgagnes	1986-

Representative of the hundreds of pre-Seaway canallers, the TRIBUNE passes through the Welland Canal in May 1986. *Jim Bartke.*

69   LAWRENCECLIFFE HALL
712'-4" x 75'-2" x 35'-7"
Davie Shipbuilding, Lauzon, QUE
April 14, 1965   Hull # 651

LAWRENCECLIFFE HALL	**1965-**
INDUSTRIAL ACCEPTANCE CORP. (HALCO)	**1965-1969**
Hall Corporation of Canada	1969-1986
Navican Management	1986-

Unloading at Conneaut, Ohio in August 1967. *Eric Hirsimaki.*

70   CHI-CHEEMAUN
365'-0" x 61'-0" x 21'-0"
Collingwood Shipyards, Collingwood, ONT
January 12, 1974   Hull # 205

CHI-CHEEMAUN	**1974-**
Ontario Department of Highways	1974-1975
THE OWEN SOUND TRANS. CO.	**1975-**

Approaching Tobermory, ONT in July 1986. *Christine Rohn Hilston.*

71   JAMES LAUGHLIN
538'-4" x 56'-2" x 32'-0"
Great Lakes Engineering Works, Ecorse, MI
April 7, 1907   Hull # 16

JAMES LAUGHLIN	**1906-1964**
Helen Evans	1964-1980
Interstate SS Co. (Hayden)	1906-1909
Interstate SS Co. (Becker)	1909-1920
Interstate SS Co. (England)	1920-1943
Interstate SS Co. (Tietjen)	1943-1949
Jones & Laughlin Steel Corp.	1949-1952
WILSON MARINE TRANSIT CO.	**1952-1964**
Hindman Transportation Co., Ltd.	1964-1979
Quebec & Ontario Trans. Co., Ltd.	1979-1980
	Sold/scrap

The LAUGHLIN is about the pass under the Aerial Bridge as she enters Duluth harbor in October 1958. *William D. Carle III.*

72 SPRING FIT OUT

It's April 1982 and the tug KINSALE is busy helping the JOSEPH H. THOMPSON out of her winter layup berth at the Nicholson Terminal in Detroit. Witnessing the event are the other members of the Hanna fleet. *Eric Hirsimaki.*

73 EDNA G
92'-5" x 23'-7" x 7'-5"
Cleveland Shipbuilding Company, Cleveland, OH
April 1, 1896   Hull # 25

EDNA G	**1896-1984**
DULUTH, MISSABE & IRON RANGE RWY	**1896-1984**
	Sold*

* Sold to the City of Two Harbors, Minnesota for display.

The EDNA G enters Duluth Harbor with a tow. *Tim Slattery.*

74 WILLIAM G. MATHER
601'-0" x 62'-0" x 27'-7"
Great Lakes Engineering Works, River Rouge, MI
May 23, 1925   Hull # 250

WILLIAM G. MATHER	**1925-**
CLEVELAND-CLIFFS SS CO.	**1925-**

The MATHER arrives in Cleveland in September 1973. *Charles Matt/Jim Semon Collection.*

75 JEAN PARISIEN
720'-0" x 75'-0" x 43'-0"
Davie Shipbuilding, Ltd., Lauzon, QUE
July 7, 1977   Hull # 684

JEAN PARISIEN	**1977-**
POWER CORP. OF CANADA, LTD. (CSL)	**1977-**

The PARISIEN is shown downbound in the Detroit River in September 1982. *Eric Hirsimaki.*

76 DIAMOND ALKALAI
580'-0" x 60'-0" x 27'-9"
Great Lakes Engineering Works, Ecorse, MI
June 1917   Hull # 166

Frank H. Goodyear	1917-1939
DIAMOND ALKALAI	**1939-1976**
Buffalo	1976-1978
Saginaw Bay	1978-1985
Buffalo SS Company (Mitchell)	1917-1922
AMERICAN SS COMPANY (B&C)	**1922-1985**
	Sold/scrap

Arriving in Cleveland, Ohio in April 1974. *Jim Semon.*

77 J. N. McWATTERS
712'-0" x 75'-3" x 34'-8"
Canadian Vickers, Ltd., Montreal, QUE
1961   Hull # 276

J. N. McWATTERS	**1961-**
MISENER TRANSPORTATION	**1961-**

Downbound near DeTour in June 1977. *David Lawler.*

78 TOM M. GIRDLER
497'-2" x 71'-7" x 27'-9"
Kaiser Company, Inc., Vancouver, WA
1945   Hull # 513

Louis McHenry Howe	1945-1951
TOM M. GIRDLER	**1951-1980**
U. S. Maritime Commission	1945-1951
Nicholson-Universal SS Co. (Browning)	1951-1952
Republic Steel Corp. (Browning)	1952-1957
REPUBLIC STEEL CORP. (WILSON)	**1957-1972**
Republic Steel Corp. (Cliffs)	1972-1980
	Sold/scrap

Lengthened 104'-0" and converted to bulk carrier in 1951.

Upbound in the St. Marys River in September 1972. *William D. Carle III.*

79 DAVID P. THOMPSON
554'-0" x 58'-2" x 33'-0"
Great Lakes Engineering Works, Ecorse, MI
June 1, 1907   Hull # 28

Wilpen	1907-1927
DAVID P. THOMPSON	**1927-1969**
Joseph S. Young	1969-1979
Shenango SS Co.	1907-1926
PIONEER SS CO. (HUTCHINSON)	**1926-1961**
American SS Co. (B&C)	1961-1979

In the Cuyahoga River in Cleveland, December 1958. *William D. Carle III.*

80 ARTHUR B. HOMER
711'-2" x 75'-1" x 33'-4"
Great Lakes Engineering Works, River Rouge, MI
November 7, 1959   Hull # 303

ARTHUR B. HOMER	**1959-1985**
BETHLEHEM STEEL CORP.	**1959-1985**
	Sold/scrap

Above the locks at the Soo in September 1978. *William D. Carle III.*

81 LAKE NIPIGON
667'-4" x 75'-0" x 32'-0"
Upper Clyde Shipbuilding, Ltd., Govan, Scotland
September 1, 1970   Hull # 101G

Temple Bar	1971-1976
LAKE NIPIGON	**1976-1984**
Laketon	1984-1986
Lake Nipigon	1986-1987
Algosound	1987-
Lambert Brothers, Ltd.	1971-1976
NIPIGON TRANSPORTATION CO. (CARRYORE)	**1976-1986**
Algoma Central Railway	1986-

Lengthened 139'-7" and converted to bulk carrier at Singapore in 1977, nicknamed "Nipigon Maru" as a result.

Downbound at Detroit in August 1977. *Dave Lawler.*

82 MANITOULIN
712'-5" x 75'-2" x 39'-3"
Davie Shipbuilding, Ltd., Lauzon, QUE
May 26, 1966   Hull # 650

MANITOULIN	**1966-**
Canada SS Lines, Ltd.	1966-1977
POWER CORPORATION OF CANADA	**1977-**
(CSL)	

The MANITOULIN passes through the Welland on a May 1986 day. *Jim Semon.*

83 McKEE SONS
620'-4" x 71'-7" x 25'-6"
Sun Shipbuilding and Drydock Co., Chester, PA
1945   Hull # 354

Marine Angel	1945-1953
McKEE SONS	**1953-**
U.S. Maritime Commission	1945-1953
AMERSAND SS CO. (B&C)	**1953-**

Lengthened 123'-0" and converted to self-unloader in 1953.

Downbound in the St. Clair River in August 1969. *Eric Hirsimaki.*

84 RALPH MISENER
720'-0" x 75'-1" x 37'-9"
Canadian Vickers, Ltd., Montreal, QUE
1967   Hull # 293

RALPH MISENER	**1967-**
SCOTT MISENER STEAMSHIPS, LTD.	**1967-**

Built as a self-unloader, but converted to a bulk freighter in 1977.

The MISENER is downbound at the Soo in November 1970. She was a unique design of self-unloader which proved a failure. The unloading gear amidships walked up and down the deck and scooped the cargo out of the hold which was one long trench. *Charles Matt/Jim Semon Collection.*

85 EUGENE W. PARGNY
580'-0" x 60'-0" x 32'-0"
American Shipbuilding Company, Lorain, OH
January 20, 1917   Hull # 719

EUGENE W. PARGNY	**1917-1984**
Pittsburgh SS Co.	1917-1952
U.S. STEEL CORP.	**1952-1981**
USS Great Lakes Fleet, Inc.	1981-Sold/scrap

A tug eases the PARGNY into the dock at the Central Furnace dock in Cleveland in August 1976. Note the Hulett's bicentennial paint scheme. *Eric Hirsimaki.*

86 BENSON FORD
596'-7" x 62'-0" x 27'-7"
Great Lakes Engineering Works, River Rouge, MI
April 26, 1924   Hull # 245

BENSON FORD	**1924-1983**
John Dykstra	1983-
FORD MOTOR CO.	**1924-1982**
Rouge Steel Company	1982-

A spring arrival in Duluth. *Tim Slattery.*

87 J. A. W. IGLEHART
486'-3" x 68'-3" x 36'-9"
Sun Shipbuilding & Drydock Company, Chester, PA
1936   Hull # 155

Pan Amoco	1936-1955
Amoco	1955-1960
H. R. Schemm	1960-1965
J. A. W. IGLEHART	**1965-**
Pan American Petroleum & Trans. Co.	1936-1943
American Oil Company	1943-1960
Boston Metals Company	1960
HURON TRANSPORTATION COMPANY	**1960-1987**
Chrysler Leasing, Inc. (Inland Lakes)	1987-

Converted to self-unloading cement carrier in 1965.

Downbound in the Detroit River in August 1969. *Eric Hirsimaki.*

88 GEORGE D. GOBLE
588'-0" x 60'-3" x 27'-7"
Toledo Shipbuilding Company, Toledo, OH
January 24, 1924   Hull # 176

William K. Field	1924-1934
Reiss Brothers	1934-1970
GEORGE D. GOBLE	**1970-1980**
Robert S. Pierson	1980-1982
Spruceglen	1982-1985
Reiss SS Company	1924-1969
Reiss SS Company (B&C)	1969-1971
Edison SS Company (B&C)	1971-1972
KINSMAN MARINE TRANSIT COMPANY	**1972-1975**
S&E Shipping Corporation	1975-1980
Pierson Steamships, Ltd.	1980-1982
P & H Shipping, Ltd.	1982-1985 Sold/scrap

The GOBLE winds her way up the Cuyahoga River in Cleveland in August 1974. *Paul A. Hilston.*

89 NORTHERN VENTURE
713'-5" x 75'-3" x 34'-5"
Kaiser Company, Portland, OR
July 15, 1944   Hull # 80

Verendrye	1944-1947
Edenfield	1947-1960
NORTHERN VENTURE	**1960-1983**
U. S. Maritime Commission	1944-1947
Edenfield Tankers, Inc.	1947-1960
NORTHERN SHIPPING (ULS)	**1960-1975**
Upper Lakes Shipping, Ltd.	1975-1983 Rebuilt*

Built as tanker. Lengthened 203'-6" and converted to bulk carrier in 1961.

* The bow and midsection of the NORTHERN VENTURE were separated from the stern and mated to a new stern to make a new boat, the CABOT, in 1983. The VENTURE's stern was then scrapped.

The NORTHERN VENTURE is unloaded at Conneaut, Ohio in August 1967. *Eric Hirsimaki.*

90   **COL. JAMES M. SCHOONMAKER**
590'-0" x 64'-2" x 34'-2"
Great Lakes Engineering Works, Ecorse, MI
July 1, 1911   Hull # 82

COL. JAMES M. SCHOONMAKER	**1911-1969**
Willis B. Boyer	1969-1987
SHENANGO FURNACE CO.	**1911-1969**
Interlake SS Co.	1969-1971
Cleveland-Cliffs SS Co.	1971-1983
American Bulk Shipping	1983-1986
Cleveland-Cliffs SS Co.	1986
	Sold*

* Sold to the City of Toledo, Ohio for display.

This stern view of the SCHOONMAKER in the open lake aptly captures the classic lines of the traditional Great Lakes bulk freighter, June 1958. *William D. Carle III.*

91   **JOHN G. MUNSON**
751'-3" x 72'-2" x 34'-5"
Manitowoc Shipbuilding Company, Manitowoc, WI
November 28, 1951   Hull # 415

JOHN G. MUNSON	**1951-**
Bradley Transportation Co.	1951-1952
U. S. STEEL CORPORATION	**1952-1981**
USS Great Lakes Fleet, Inc.	1981-

Lengthened 102'-0" in 1976.

Entering Duluth Harbor on a wintery day. *Tim Slattery.*

92   **WLI-602 - USCGC BUCKTHORN**
100'-0" x 24'-0" x ?
Mobile Ship Repair, Inc., Mobile, AL
1963   Hull #

BUCKTHORN	**1963-**
U. S. COAST GUARD	**1963-**

Downbound near DeTour in June 1977. Buoy tenders like the BUCKTHORN play an important role in keeping the shipping lanes safe. *Dave Lawler.*

93   **E. J. NEWBERRY**
589'-2" x 60'-0" x 27'-7"
Great Lakes Engineering Works, River Rouge, MI
April 4, 1925   Hull # 249

William C. Atwater	1925-1936
E. J. Kulas	1936-1953
Ben Moreell	1953-1955*
Thomas E. Millsop	1955-1976
E. J. NEWBERRY	**1976-1982**
Cedarglen	1982-
Wilson Transit Co.	1925-1955
National Steel Corp. (Hanna)	1955-1976
Reoch Transports, Ltd./Robert	
Pierson Holdings (Soo River)	1976-1977
PIERSON STEAMSHIPS, LTD.	**1977-1982**
(SOO RIVER)	
P&H Shipping, Ltd.	1982-

* In 1955 the Albert E. Heekin and Louis W. Hill were traded to Wilson by National Steel for the BEN MOREELL.

This boat was the first on the Great Lakes to have an "iron deckhand" (hatch crane). Twilight ends another day at Huron, Ohio in August 1978, though the NEWBERRY continues to load grain. *Jim Semon.*

94   **MEDUSA CHALLENGER**
530'-0" x 56'-2" x 32'-0"
Great Lakes Engineering Works, Ecorse, MI
February 17, 1906   Hull # 17

William P. Snyder	1906-1926
Elton Hoyt II	1926-1952
Alexander D. Chisholm	1952-1966
MEDUSA CHALLENGER	**1966-**
Shenango Furnace Co.	1906-1929
Youngstown SS Co. (Interlake)	1929-1930
Interlake SS Co.	1930-1966
CEMENT TRANSIT CO. (MEDUSA)	**1966-**

Converted to a self-unloading cement carrier in 1967.

The CHALLENGER is winding her way upriver in the Cuyahoga River at Cleveland in October 1985. *Eric Hirsimaki.*

95   **GEORGE M. STEINBRENNER**
556'-2" x 56'-4" x 26'-5"
West Bay City Shipbuilding Co., W. Bay City, MI
October 7, 1907   # 76

Arthur H. Hawgood	1907-1911
Joseph Block	1911-1969
GEORGE M. STEINBRENNER	**1969-1979**
Neptune SS Co. (Hawgood)	1907-1911
Inland Steel Co. (Hutchinson)	1911-1957
Inland Steel Co.	1957-1968
Lake Shipping, Inc. (Am. Shpbld'g Co.)	1968-1969
KINSMAN MARINE TRANSIT CO.	**1969-1975**
S&E Shipping Corp.	1975
	Sold/scrap

Downbound on the St. Clair River in August 1969. *Eric Hirsimaki.*

96   **STUART J. CORT**
989'-3" x 105'-0" x 44'-9"
Erie Marine, Inc., Erie, PA
April 1, 1972   Hull # 101

STUART J. CORT	**1972-**
BETHLEHEM STEEL CORP.	**1972-**

The midsection of the CORT was built in Erie and the bow and stern in Pascagoula, Mississippi. They formed what was known as "stubby," seen in the insert, which sailed to Erie and was cut apart and the midsection added. August 1970. *Eric Hirsimaki.* The CORT, the first 1,000 footer, is upbound in the St. Marys River in September 1972. *William D. Carle III.*

97   **VIKING**
347'-0" x 56'-2" x 19'-2"
Manitowoc Shipbuilding Company, Manitowoc, WI
1925   Hull # 214

Ann Arbor No. 7	1925-1964
VIKING	**1964-**
ANN ARBOR RAILROAD COMPANY	**1925-1983**
Peterson Builders, Inc.	1983-

The VIKING approaches her birthplace, Manitowoc, Wisconsin, in May 1980. *G. W. Deucher.*

98 WILFRED SYKES
661'-1" x 70'-2" x 32'-3"
American Shipbuilding Company, Lorain, OH
June 28, 1949   Hull # 866

WILFRED SYKES	**1949-**
Inland Steel Corp. (Hutchinson)	1949-1957
INLAND STEEL CORPORATION	**1957-**

Converted to self-unloader in 1975.

The SYKES is shown at Lorain in early 1949 prior to her launching. *Raymond A. Rohn.*

99 MIDNIGHT PASSAGE

The JOSEPH H. THOMPSON is downbound in lock #1. While she is being lowered to the Lake Huron level the ST. CLAIR, which has followed her down the lake from Superior, works her way down the upper piers into lock #2. It's midnight and only a few people are paying much attention to this September 1982 scene. *Eric Hirsimaki.*

100 THE INTERNATIONAL
586'-3" x 60'-2" x 28'-0"
American Shipbuilding Company, Lorain, OH
April 24, 1923   Hull # 784

William H. Warner	1923-1934
THE INTERNATIONAL	**1934-1977**
Maxine	1977-1982
J. F. Vaughn	1982
Oakglen	1982-
Panda SS Company (Tomlinson)	1923-1934
INTERNATIONAL HARVESTER COMPANY	**1934-1977**
WSC Corporation	1977-1979
WSC Shipping, Inc.	1979-1981
Triad Salvage Company	1981
Pierson Steamships, Ltd.	1981-1982
P & H Shipping, Ltd.	1982

For many years THE INTERNATIONAL and her sister, THE HARVESTER, carried the colors of their namesake company. The former arrives in South Chicago, IL in May 1975. *Jim Bartke.*

101 HERBERT C. JACKSON
670'-6" x 75'-1" x 33'-0"
Great Lakes Engineering Works, Ecorse, MI
February 20, 1959   Hull # 302

HERBERT C. JACKSON	**1959-**
Interlake SS Company (PM)	1959-1966
Pickands Mather & Company	1966-1973
Interlake SS Company (PM)	1973-1986
Interlake SS Company	1986

Converted to self-unloader in 1975.

The JACKSON pushes her way through some ice during an early season arrival in Duluth. She will probably load ore at the DM&IR dock, no doubt the captain's hoping there isn't an ice buildup at the Soo on the downbound trip. *Tim Slattery.*

102 SOODOC
342'-0" x 49'-0" x 27'-0"
Collingwood Shipyards, Collingwood, ONT
April 19, 1976   Hull # 210

SOODOC	**1976-**
N. M. PATTERSON & SONS, LTD.	**1976-**

At Port Weller, Ontario in May 1984. *Jim Bartke.*

103 CASON J. CALLAWAY
727'-4" x 70'-2" x 31'-3"
Great Lakes Engineering Works, River Rouge, MI
March 22, 1952   Hull # 297

CASON J. CALLAWAY	**1952-**
Pittsburgh SS Company	1952
U. S. STEEL CORPORATION	**1952-1981**
USS Great Lakes Fleet, Inc.	1981-

Lengthened 120'-0" in 1974. Converted to self-unloader in 1982.

The CALLAWAY, fully loaded, departs Duluth. This low angle stern view makes her seem even bigger. *Tim Slattery.*

104 ROBERT C. NORTON
603'-8" x 60'-2" x 30'-2"
Great Lakes Engineering Works, Ashtabula, OH
1943   Hull # 525

Pilot Knob 2nd	1943
Steelton	1943-1966
Frank Purnell	1966-1974
ROBERT C. NORTON	**1974-**
U.S. Maritime Commission	1943
Bethlehem Transportation Co.	1943-1966
Interlake SS Company	1966
Pickands Mather & Company	1966-1974
OGLEBAY NORTON COMPANY (COLUMBIA)	**1974-**

Converted to self-unloader in 1966.

At the stone dock in Huron, Ohio. August 1978. *Jim Semon.*

105 WALTER A. STERLING
716'-5" x 75'-2" x 34'-4"
Bethlehem Shipbldg & Drydock Co., Sparrows Pt., MD
December 20, 1942   Hull # 4378

Chiwawa	1942-1961
WALTER A. STERLING	**1961-1985**
William Clay Ford	1985-
Socony Vacuum Oil Company	1942-1947
Cities Service Oil Company	1947-1960
CLEVELAND-CLIFFS SS COMPANY	**1960-1985**
Rouge Steel Company	1985-

Lengthened 228'-3" and converted from tanker to bulk freighter in 1961. Lengthened 96'-0" in 1976. Converted to self-unloader in 1978.

The STERLING backs out of Huron, Ohio after being unloaded in September 1972. *Charles Matt/Jim Semon Collection.*

106 DAWN OF A NEW DAY

Photographer *Tim Slattery* captured much of the beauty of the lakes in this scene of a self-unloader clearing Duluth early one morning.

107 TROISDOC
253'-6" x 43'-9" x 22'-6"
Canadian Shpbldng & Engrng, Ltd., Collingwood, ONT
June 4, 1955   Hull # 151

Iroquois	1955-1967
TROISDOC	**1967-1983**

Canada Steamship Lines, Ltd.	1955-1967
N. M. PATERSON & SONS, LTD.	**1967-1983**
	Sold*

* Sold to Mexican interests.

The TROISDOC was one of last "canallers" built, i.e., boats that operated on the St. Lawrence River prior to the Seaway. She's shown at Huron, Ohio in October 1978 loading grain. *Jim Semon.*

108 MARKHAM
316'-0" x 62'-0" x 28'-0"
Avondale Marine Works, Inc., Avondale, LA
June 10, 1959   Hull # 904

MARKHAM — 1959-

U.S. ARMY CORPS OF ENGINEERS — 1959-

The MARKHAM dredges material from the harbor bottom by means of a suction head suspended on a long pipe alongside. Dredgings are placed in a hopper contained in the boat. When it was full, the MARKHAM would sail into the lake and open the hopper, allowing the dredged material to fall to the lake bottom. *Jim Semon.*

109 IRVING S. OLDS
622'-6" x 67'-2" x 30'-3"
American Shipbuilding Company, Lorain, OH
May 22, 1942   Hull # 825

IRVING S. OLDS — 1942-

Pittsburgh SS Company	1942-1952
U.S. STEEL CORPORATION	**1952-1981**
USS Great Lakes Fleet, Inc.	1981-

The OLDS is about the enter Duluth Harbor in August 1980. *Eric Hirsimaki.*

110 CITY OF MIDLAND 41
389'-2" x 58'-2" x 20'-5"
Manitowoc Shipbuilding Company, Manitowoc, WI
1941   Hull # 311

CITY OF MIDLAND 41 — 1941-

Pere Marquette Railroad	1941-1947
CHESAPEAKE & OHIO RAILWAY	**1947-1983**
Michigan-Wisconsin Transportation Co.	1983-

Arriving in Ludington, MI in September 1980. *G. W. Deucher.*

111 JOHN P. REISS
504'-0" x 54'-0" x 30'-0"
American Shipbuilding Company, Lorain, OH
January 29, 1910   Hull # 377

JOHN P. REISS — 1910-1972

REISS SS COMPANY	**1910-1969**
Reiss SS Company (B&C)	1969-1971
Edison SS Company (B&C)	1971-1972
Kinsman Marine Transit Company	1972
	Sold/scrap

Downbound in Whitefish Bay in September 1966. *Eric Hirsimaki.*

112 MEETING ABOVE THE SOO

The GEORGE M. HUMPHREY meets an Amoco tanker above the Upper Piers at the Soo. The tanker will soon be in Lake Superior whereas the HUMPHREY will spend most of this October 1981 day in the rivers where at least there will be something to see. *Eric Hirsimaki.*

Rear Cover   PERPETUAL MOTION

There's one thing about the lake boats, they never stop moving. They operate 24 hours a day and to anchor for even a few hours is costly. For this reason the loading and unloading docks also work around the clock. This scene at the Norfolk & Western Railway's Huron, Ohio dock catches the Huletts during the dock crew's midnight "lunch" break. September 1982. *Lloyd D. Lewis.*

INDEX OF BOATS

ALGOWEST	46, 47
ALPENA	40
ANCHORED FOR FOG	62
ANDREWS, MATTHEW	43
ASHLAND	41
BAYTON	57
BLOCK, L. E.	26
BOYER, WILLIS B.	30, 90*
BROOKDALE	34
BUCKTHORN	92
BURTON, COURTNEY	67
CALLAWAY, CASON J.	103
CANADIAN PROSPECTOR	63
CHICAGO TRIBUNE	68
CHI-CHEEMAUN	70
CHIEF WAWATAM	35
CITY OF MIDLAND 41	110
COLLISION BEND (T. W. LAMONT)	17
CORT, STUART J.	96
DAWN OF A NEW DAY	106
DELANCEY, WILLIAM J.	27
DES GROSSILIERS	58
DIAMOND ALKYLAI	76
DULUTH HARBOR	36
EDNA G	73
ELMDALE	45
ERIE QUEEN	29
EVANS, HELEN	37, 71*
FOLLOW THE LEADER	65
FORD, BENSON	86
FORD, E. M.	33
FORT YORK	42
FRONTENAC	32
GIRDLER, TOM M.	78
GOBLE, GEORGE D.	88
GREENE, EDWARD. B.	50
HEEKIN, ALBERT E.	22
HINDMAN, GEORGE	53
HOMER, ARTHUR B.	80
HOYT, ELTON 2nd	48
HUMPHREY, GEORGE M.	112
IGLEHART, J. A. W.	87
JACKSON, HERBERT C.	101
JONES, B. F.	10
LAKE NIPIGON	81
LAKEWOOD	21
LaLIBERTE, HENRY	24
LAMONT, THOMAS W.	17
LAUGHLIN, JAMES	71, 37*
LAWRENCECLIFFE HALL	69
LEHIGH	31
L'ORME #1	54
MANITOULIN	82
MARKHAM	108
MATHER, WILLIAM G.	74
McCULLOUGH, JOAN M.	28
McKEE SONS	83
McWATTERS, J. N.	77
MEDUSA CHALLENGER	94
MEET ABOVE THE SOO	112
MERCURY	23
MIDNIGHT PASSAGE (JOSEPH H. THOMPSON)	99
MISENER, RALPH	84
MUNSON, JOHN G.	91
NEWBERRY, E. J.	93
NORISLE	19
NORTHERN VENTURE	89
NORTON, ROBERT C.	104
OLDS, IRVING S.	109
PARGNY, EUGENE M.	85
PARISIEN, JEAN	75
REISS, JOHN P.	111
RHODE ISLAND	14
ROESCH, WILLIAM R.	39
RYERSON, EDWARD L.	44
SCHOONMAKER, COL. JAMES M.	90, 30*
SCHWAB, CHARLES M.	15
SEAWAY QUEEN	12
SHARON	51
SILVER ISLE	9
SOODOC	102
SOUTH AMERICAN	66
SPEER, EDGAR B.	11
SPRING FIT-OUT	72
STEINBRENNER, GEORGE M.	95
STEPHENSON, GEORGE	49
STERLING, WALTER A.	105
"Stubby" (STUART J. CORT)	96
SUNRISE IN DULUTH	25
SYKES, WILFRED	98
THE CLEVELANDER	16
THE INTERNATIONAL	100
THOMPSON, DAVID P.	79
THOMPSON, JOSEPH H.	60, 61, 99, back cover
TOMLINSON, G. A.	56
TROISDOC	107
UHLMAN BROTHERS	64
UNGAVA TRANSPORT	18
VIKING	97
WATSON, RALPH H.	55
WHITNEY, WILLIAM A.	20
WILSON, CHARLES E.	13
WILTRANCO I	59
WINTER RUN (E. B. SPEER)	11
WOLVERINE	52

*Same vessel under another name

TYPICAL 1,000 FT. SELF-UNLOADER AS BUILT BY AMSHIP

Length — 1,005 feet overall
Height — 115 feet overall
Beam (Width) — 105 feet overall
Depth — 50 feet
Draft — 28 feet
Engines — Two diesels, each 8,000 brake horsepower
Propellers — Two variable pitch
Speed — 16 mph loaded, 17 mph light
Capacity — 59,000 tons of iron ore pellets, 52,000 tons of coal
Unloading — 10,000 tons of iron ore pellets per hour, 6,000 tons of coal per hour
Bow Thruster — 1,500 horsepower
Fuel — 152,000 gallons for propulsion, 31,000 gallons for generators
Electrical Power — four 800 KW, 480-volt diesel generators
Hatches — 36 — each 65 feet long, 11 feet wide, 5¼ tons each
Holds — Seven

Mid-Ship Section

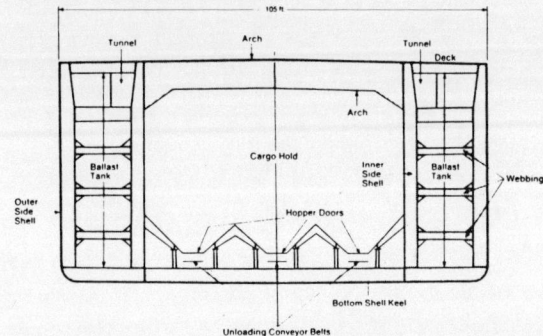

1,000 FOOTER — BUILT 1976-1981
CAPACITY: 59,000 TONS

730 FOOTER — BUILT 1952-1972
CAPACITY: 25,000 TONS

600 FOOTER — BUILT 1906-1943
CAPACITY: 14,000 TONS

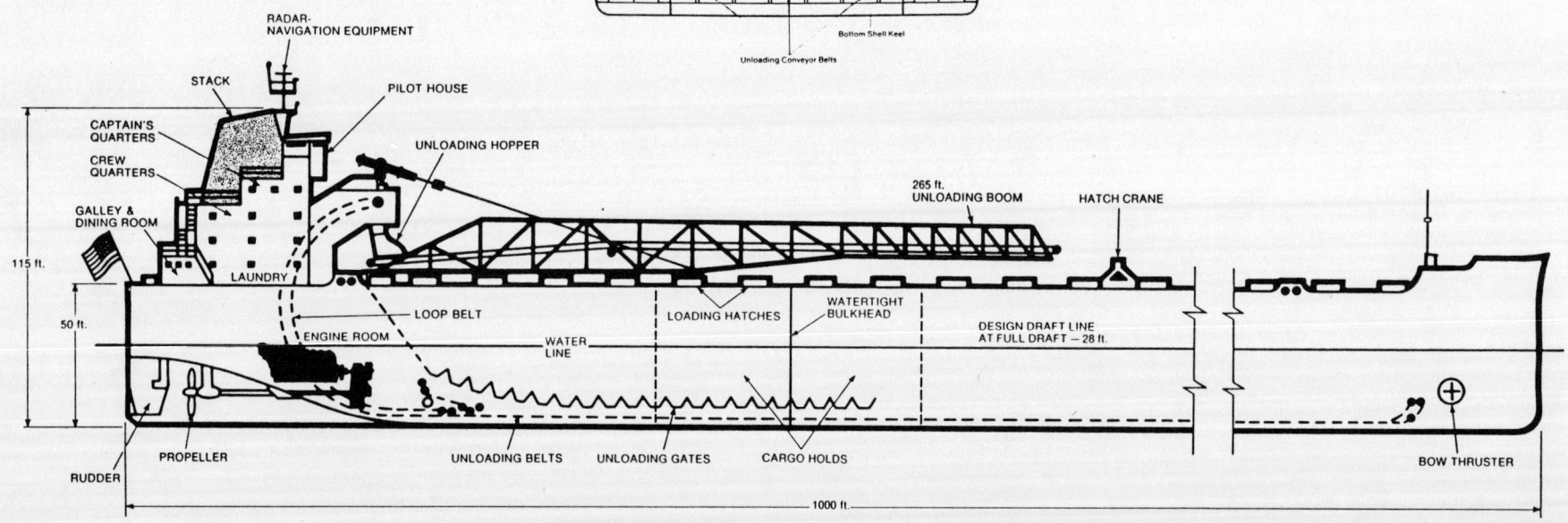

The traditional Great Lakes straight-deck bulk freighter has been superseded by the 1,000 foot self-unloader. The boat shown above is the type built by the American Shipbuilding Co. at Lorain, OH. Four have been built:

JAMES R. BARKER	(1,005 ft.)	— 1976
MISSABI MINER	(1,005 ft.)	— 1977
GEORGE A. STINSON	(1,005 ft.)	— 1978
WM. J. DeLANCEY	(1,013 ft.)	— 1981